Verses World

Original Verses for Greetings Cards

by

Paula Perro

First published 2015

Copyright © Paula Perro 2015

The right of Paula Perro to be identified as the author of this book has been asserted in accordance with Section 77 and 78 of the Copyrights, Designs and Patents Act 1988. Copying of this manuscript, in whole or in part, without the written permission of the author or his publisher is strictly prohibited and would constitute a breach of copyright held.

Contents

Funny Birthday Poems 7

Traditional Birthday Card Verses 11

Family Birthday Verses...................................13

    Birthday Card Verses for Mums..................13

    Birthday Card Verses for Dads 14

    Birthday Verses for Sons or Daughters.....................14

    Birthday Verses for Daughters 15

    Birthday Verses for Sons 16

    Happy Birthday Brother 17

    Happy Birthday Sister.................................17

    Birthday Poems for Wives..........................17

    Birthday Poems for Husbands....................18

Funny Christmas Poems..................................19

Traditional Christmas Card Verses................23

Christmas Card Verses for the Family 27

    Christmas Card Poems for Dad 27

    Christmas Card Poems for Mum 27

    Happy Christmas Daughter Poems 28

    Happy Christmas Son Poems 28

- Christmas Card Poem for Son/Daughter and Daughter/Son-in-law 29
- Christmas Card Verses for Wife or Husband 30
- Christmas Card Verses for Granddaughter 32
- Funny Thanksgiving Poems 34
- Funny Valentine Poems 36
  - Funny valentine poems from a girl to a guy: 40
  - Funny Valentine Poems for wife 41
  - Funny Valentine Poems for husband 42
  - Poems for wife or husband 42
- Sentimental Mother's Day Poems 43
- Funny Mother's Day Poems 49
- Funny Father's Day Poems 50
- Sentimental Father's Day Poems 52
- Funny Easter Verses 53
- Religious Easter Poems 55
- Get Well Soon Poems 56
- Thank You Poems 58
  - General Poems to say Thank You 58
  - Birthday Gift Thank you 58
  - Thank you for looking after my pet 60
  - Poem to say thank you for your hospitality 61
- Teacher Appreciation Poems 62

A poem for a Maths Teacher 62

A poem for an English / Poetry Teacher 62

A Poem for a Science Teacher....................63

A poem for a History Teacher 63

A poem for an Art Teacher.........................63

A poem for a French Teacher....................64

A poem for a Spanish Teacher 64

General Teacher Appreciation Poems 65

Funny Wedding Anniversary Poems 66

Funny Wedding Anniversary Poems for a husband or wife 66

Funny Wedding Anniversary Poems for a couple 68

Sentimental Wedding Anniversary Poems 69

Sentimental Anniversary Poems for a husband or wife 69

Sentimental Wedding Anniversary Poems for a couple 70

Funny Retirement Verses.............................71

Sentimental Retirement Verses 74

Good Luck Poems...75

General Good Luck Poems 75

Good Luck For Exams 76

For a job Interview 77

For a New Job..78

Funny Birthday Poems

You're known and respected
For your love of thrift,
And so, to honour this, I have
Not got you a gift.

~~~

There is a world record that
I think that you will break
Sometime in the next few years -
It's "candles on a cake."

~~~

You've had many, many birthdays,
Too many for me to mention,
But there are still one or two more
Before you start your pension.

It's your birthday, yet again,
I hope you have a ball.
I know you won't be shocked to hear
I've got you bugger all.

~~~

Last year- twenty candles,
That does not sound a lot.
But that was not the whole cake,
Just on the slice I got.

~~~

Let's celebrate your birthday.
Let's drink 'til we fall over.
Let's try not to think about
Tomorrow's big hangover.

~~~

I believe team name will win the league.
I believe climate change will work out fine.
I believe every politician's promise.
I believe that you are twenty nine.

Getting old is no fun
Don't let it make you cross.
Have a few beers and soon
You will not give a toss.

~~~

People laugh at us and say
"Look at those old farts,
They're from the past, a time when
Greensleeves was in the charts."
I may have said this once before
But I'll say it again.
The good old days were better -
We were younger then!

~~~

Let's celebrate your birthday,
We're young, for heaven's sake!
Perhaps too old for clubbing,
But not too old for cake.

"The man who has everything"
That's what everyone says.
I guess it must be all those gifts
From all your many birthdays.

~~~

Becoming old's an awful thing,
It really breaks my heart.
You get your head together, and
Your body falls apart.

~~~

Becoming old is miserable
It's really very sad.
I wonder at what age you start
To dance just like your dad?

~~~

Who cares how old you are?
Let's leave your age unspoken.
Hope you get the gifts you want -
Pipe, slippers, and book token.

Traditional Birthday Card Verses

Here's a wish for someone dear
And very special too -
Happy Birthday ...name
And lots of love to you.

~~~

Here's wishing you a lovely day
That leaves you feeling good.
I hope it brings the special things
A happy birthday should.

~~~

Here's a little birthday card
That's being sent your way
To bring you lots of wishes
For happiness today.

~~~

This card comes to tell you
In case you didn't know,
How special you will always be

To those who love you so.
Hoping that this greeting
Will lovingly convey
Just how much you mean
Today and every day.

~~~

Today's a really special day
Because your birthday's here
And you're someone who brings a smile
To each day of the year.

~~~

The message in this card contains
A birthday wish for you.
You're someone who means so much
Today and all year through.

~~~

This message is for someone
Who's as special as can be,
You are a really precious
Member of our family.

Family Birthday Verses

Birthday Card Verses for Mums

Mum is a word that says so much
It has a happy, special touch.
It means caring and sharing - loving too,
The kind of word made just for you

~~~

A touch of class,
A certain style,
A caring heart,
A loving smile,
A great mum,
A good friend too,
So many things,
To love about you.

You brighten up my life,
With tender love and care,
Whenever I need you
I know that you'll be there.
You're someone I can count on,
That's why I want to say
Thanks for being my mum,
Here's to your special day.

Birthday Card Verses for Dads

I was going to write a poem about your age,
With cruel jokes and insulting stuff.
Then I remembered that you have me,
And I figured you've suffered enough.

Birthday Verses for Sons or Daughters

You're clever and you're charming
We've known it all along.
You're handsome, cool, and talented,
Where could all that be from?

Because today's your birthday
It's time to celebrate
So here's a "Happy Birthday"
To someone really great.

Birthday Verses for Daughters

You're clever and you're beautiful
We've known it all along.
You're funny, kind, and talented,
Where could all that be from?

~~~

Here's hoping your birthday brings
Lots and lots of lovely things.

When it comes to Daughters
There're lots of them about
But you're the very, very best
Of that, there is no doubt

Birthday Verses for Sons

Many years ago,
I had a son.
I had no idea,
It would be so much fun.
A beautiful baby,
Alas, no more.
Happy Birthday young man,
You've a world to explore.

~~~

You're really very special
When all is said and done
A very happy birthday
To a very special son

Happy Birthday Brother

I just wanted to tell you,
On this, your special day,
I'm glad that you're my brother,
Despite what others say.

Happy Birthday Sister

I recall when you were young,
Let me reminisce.
Now you're very, very old.
Happy Birthday, Sis

Birthday Poems for Wives

Happy Birthday to
The world's most perfect wife.
I feel so very lucky
To have you in my life.

You're sexy and you're lovely
You're really, really hot.
This card says happy birthday,
I fancy you a lot.

Birthday Poems for Husbands

I love the time I spend with you
I just can't get enough.
You're handsome and you're charming,
You're also pretty buff!

Funny Christmas Poems

I like being friends with you, and I
Find your company pleasant.
I hope this means a lot because
I've not got you a present.

~~~

No socks, no tie, no DVD,
And no Samsung Galaxy,
No gold, no frankincense, no myrrh
No gift from me at all this year.

~~~

When Santa saw your Christmas list
He said "Ho Ho Ho!"
I asked if you'd been good this year,
He said "No No No!"

~~~

Chestnuts roasting on an open fire,
Sprouts are boiling in the pan,
I wonder if this year you'll get
A sweater from your gran.

A wish for festive jollity -
That's your Christmas gift from me.
I know, "that's cheap" I hear you moan,
But I can't afford a new smartphone.

~~~

Here's a Christmas story for you,
You probably won't believe.
I bumped into old Santa Claus
Last year, on Christmas Eve.
I saw him up on my roof
Parking up his sled.
He gave me a message for you,
This is what he said -
"name has been naughty again,
Next year is his/her last chance.
Next year I am going to
Take a tougher stance."
I meant to pass the message on
But I did not remember.
Sorry there's not much of the year left,
Just half of December.

I hope the Christmas spirit
Brings you joy and cheer
And when the spirit's finished
Get started on the beer!

~~~

I hope this Christmas brings you
Fantastic festive fun,
Good will, peace, and joy,
And pressies by the ton!

~~~

Be happy and jolly
At this time of year.
Be nice to all the people you
Don't usually go near.

May your stuffing be tasty
May your turkey plump,
May your potatoes and gravy
Have nary a lump.
May your yams be delicious
And your pies take the prize,
And may your Christmas dinner
Stay off your thighs!

Traditional Christmas Card Verses

Christmas is coming
And guess what it brings?
Lots of surprises and
The happiest of things.

~~~

Christmas is coming,
The rush has begun.
Looking for presents
That bring so much fun.

~~~

There's holly and tinsel
And presents galore.
Bright decorations
And cards by the score.

This Christmas card comes
With love from me to you.
Because you mean so much
And are loved all year through.

~~~

Now that it is Christmas time
This greeting comes to say
That you are always thought of
In a warm and loving way.

~~~

Now that Christmas time is here
This greeting comes to you
To wish you every happiness
In everything you do.

There's joyfulness and meaning
In every festive song
It makes the world seem brighter
When Christmas comes along
And all the old traditions
Make our hearts and faces glow
When we recall the Christmases
We knew so long ago

~~~

At this festive time of year
This comes to let you know
You're always in the hearts and minds
Of those who love you so

~~~

This greeting comes to wish you
At this festive time of year
A wealth of joy and happiness
And hearts so full of cheer

Wishing you a merry
Festive holiday,
And hope you have a very
Happy Christmas Day.

Christmas Card Verses for the Family

Christmas Card Poems for Dad

The turkeys are nervous
But dad's more nervous still -
Worried about the Christmas
Credit card bill.
I just want to say that
I do appreciate
Everything you do for me,
I think you're really great.

Christmas Card Poems for Mum

You bring a little magic
When Christmas time is here.
I don't know how you do it but
You do it every year.
I just want to say thank you,
For all the things you do
Not only at Christmas time
But for the whole year through

Happy Christmas Daughter Poems

You're such a perfect daughter
You're gorgeous, kind, and sweet.
You make each day so lovely.
You make Christmas complete.
You're funny and you're clever,
You're wise and thoughtful too.
So this is just a little verse
To say that we love you.

Happy Christmas Son Poems

Do not forget to hang your stocking up.
That's just a little reminder for you.
While we're on the subject, since it's Christmas,
Please tidy your other stuff away too.

Christmas Card Poem for Son/Daughter and Daughter/Son-in-law

You're such a perfect son/daughter
No-one could ask for more
And thanks to you, now I have
A perfect son/daughter-in-law.
Having you nearby
To share this festive day
Is something to be treasured
In a very special way

~~~

Inside this card
Comes not one wish, but two.
For you both mean so much
And are loved all year through.

Christmas Card Verses for Wife or Husband

Christmas time is hectic
And there's such a lot to do
But I'm still really happy
'Cos I share it all with you.

~~~

Christmas time with you is
A time I would not miss.
Let's hang a sprig of mistletoe
And seal it with a kiss.

~~~

So here's a wish at Christmas
To hope that it will be
As lovely and as special
As you always are to me!

Ever since we married
You've made my dreams come true.
So all I need for Christmas
Is mistletoe and you.

~~~

We'll curl up on the sofa
With Christmas stars above
We'll give each other presents
And drink a toast to love.

~~~

As long as we're together
I'm happy as can be,
Christmas with my wife/husband
Sounds pretty good to me.

Christmas Card Verses for Granddaughter

Christmas time reminds us all
How wonderful you are.
A Granddaughter, an angel,
A shining Christmas star.

~~~

You brighten up the winter
With everything you do.
And Christmas time is perfect
With a little girl like you.

~~~

You'll make each moment magical
And with your cheeky smile
You'll bring that extra sparkle
That makes life so worthwhile.

You're the icing on the cake,
The fairy on the tree.
Loved and treasured very much
The way you'll always be.

Funny Thanksgiving Poems

I love the Thanksgiving feast when
The prayer has been said and we've blessed it,
And all that remains is to eat,
Then lie down and slowly digest it.

~~~

I love the turkey and stuffing
The cranberry sauce is yummy.
I love it how they make their way
Down into my tummy.

~~~

A Thanksgiving rhyme to help you remember
Which Thursday it is, in November.
Apart from in Canada to the north,
It always occurs on the fourth.

~~~

Thanksgiving's been a tradition
Since 1863
It's nice for everyone involved
Unless you are a turkey.

On Thanksgiving Day if you
Want to start a riot,
Go up to the cook and say
That you are on a diet.

Funny Valentine Poems

Some girls do not need flowers from their man,
Some girls complain that chocolates make them fat,
Some girls do not need big romantic gestures,
Please be advised that I am not like that!

~~~

Facebook says I'm single
But that's not really true.
My heart belongs to someone,
And that someone is you.
We'd make a great couple,
Jealous folk would hate us,
So please give me a reason
To update my status.

~~~

Take me somewhere nice tonight
We'll have a cosy chat,
Any place that doesn't ask,
'Do you want fries with that?'

~~~

On Valentine's day
This is just a note to say
I'm glad I married you,
And I bet the kids are, too

~~~

I am your mystery valentine,
Your secret admirer.
I'm rich, good-looking, sexy,
And a compulsive liar.

~~~

I love when we're together.
I miss you when we're not -
My heart fills with sadness,
My nose fills with snot.

If I were a knight, for you
I'd slay a mighty beast.
If I were a chef, for you
I would prepare a feast.
If I were a poet, for you
I would write a sonnet.
But, I'm not, so here, for you
Is a card with a love heart on it.

~~~

Your love is worth more to me
Than diamonds, gold, and rubies.
I love your lips,
Your waist, your hips,
Your eyes, your legs, your boobies.

~~~

You're such a red hot sexy guy/chick
You really blow my mind.
You are the guy/girl of my dreams
The hot and saucy kind.

You're gorgeous, smart, and sexy,
You're as special as can be.
Sometimes I wonder what the hell
Are you doing with me?

~~~

You're such a very sexy girl
It has to be be a crime.
But that's okay because I am
Prepared to do hard time.

~~~

Some people go for looks,
Some personality,
Some people go for brains,
I went for all three.

~~~

You are a very sexy guy/girl
You make my heart go potty.
I can see the one for me
Is you, cause you're top totty!

Funny valentine poems from a girl to a guy:

I love you, I love you, more than you know,
I love you more than Juliet loved Romeo.

I love you, I love you, I'll say it again,
I love you, more than Barbie loves Ken.

I love you, I love you, I love you more than
Catherine Zeta Jones loves her old man.

I love you, I love you, I love you so
I'll be your Princess Leia if you'll be my Han Solo.

... and here's a variation from a guy to a girl:

I love you, I love you, more than you know,
More than Joe DiMaggio loved Marilyn Monroe.

I love you, I love you, I'll say it again,
I love you, more than Superman loves Lois Lane.

I love you, I love you, I'm hit by Cupid's arrow,
I love you more than King Kong loved Ann Darrow.

I love you, I love you, I love you so
Be my Esmerelda, I'll be your Quasimodo.

Funny Valentine Poems for wife

Tons of love
Loads of kisses
I'm so glad
That you're my missus

Funny Valentine Poems for husband

Tons of love
Loads of kisses
I'm so glad
That I'm your missus

You are a gorgeous sexy man,
I'm glad that you're my hubby,
But don't worry, I'll still love you
When you're bald and tubby.

Poems for wife or husband

Roses are red
Violets are blue
I'm so glad
I married you.

Sentimental Mother's Day Poems

There's something that I need to say
So that you know for sure -
No-one in the whole wide world
Could ever love you more.

~~~

Parenthood's a full time job
With little chance to rest
But being a lovely mother
Is what you do best

~~~

A mother is the dearest friend of all.
She cares with all her heart
She helps with problems big and small
She's loved you from the start

~~~

When it comes to Mothers
There's lots of them about
But you're the very, very best
Of that, there is no doubt

A Love like no other
Is the love of a Mother
A mother is a friend
on whom you can depend

~~~

You really are the perfect blend
My mother, and my bestest friend.

~~~

Mum's a word that means so much
It has a happy, special touch -
Caring, sharing, loving too,
The kind of word just made for you.

~~~

The day that God was making mums
It's clear that I was blessed,
Because the mum he gave me was
The very, very best.

Any time I need you mum
I know that you'll be there
With good advice and common sense
And lots of love to spare.

~~~

You really are the perfect Mum
And I hope that you can see
That even if I don't say it much
You mean the world to me

~~~

I want to say this Mother's Day
That nothing can compare
To the wonderful relationship
That we will always share

~~~

If mothers could be bought and sold
Just like stocks and shares,
Those wise enough to invest in you
Would all be millionaires.

For all the understanding
You show the whole year through
For all your care and guidance
I give my thanks to you

~~~

Fee! Fie! Foe! Fum!
I'm so glad that you're my mum!

~~~

Although I may not tell you
quite as often as I should,
This wish brings all the gratitude
A message ever could

~~~

I'm really very glad
To have you as my ma.
You are the very best one
In the world, by far.

Here's to you on Mother's Day
For all the things you do.
This special wish is bringing
Love and thanks to you!

~~~

You bring your gentle goodness
To everything you touch
And I will always love you -
You'll never know how much

~~~

Mum you taught me all I know.
Perhaps you thought I hadn't heard
The lessons and advice you gave,
But I heard every word.
Because you thought I'd carry on
And go my own sweet way
The truth is, mum your good advice
Comes back to me each day
With every year that passed by
I've come to realize
You're not just an amazing mum
You're also very wise
You have made me
The person I am today
And I carry your words with me
Every day.

Funny Mother's Day Poems

You taught me how to wash my face
And how to use the potty.
You made me eat up all my greens
And wiped my nose when snotty.
You taught me to be nice and kind
And even to be funny.
You taught me to say Please and Thanks
So 'Please' can I borrow some money?
'Thanks'.

~~~

I just want to say
I'm glad you are my mother,
And that I forgive you
For my little brother.

~~~

When I was born I drooled and belched
And made smells that were bad.
But I grew up and stopped all that,
So why the hell can't dad?

Funny Father's Day Poems

I know it can't be easy
Sometimes I drive you mad
But I want you to know
I'm happy you're my dad.

~~~

They say the apple never falls
Far from the tree.
Let's spend a moment looking at
This analogy.
I'm quite clearly the apple;
The tree - that must be you.
This means that you're the one to blame
For everything I do!

~~~

This Father's Day card
Is just for you, to say,
You are the best dad ever.
Three cheers for you! Hooray!

I could have bought you socks,
Or a bottle of beer, or three,
But you don't really need those things
You're lucky, you have me!

~~~

To honour your greatness
I give you the award -
"Dad of the year".
It's all I can afford.

~~~

You taught me how to ride a bike,
You're really very clever.
You taught me lots and lots of things.
You are the best dad ever.

~~~

Great huge massive hugs.
You're so the best, you are!
Most awesome dad ever -
An all-round superstar!

Sentimental Father's Day Poems

Thank you for the fun times,
The laughter that we share.
Thanks for always listening,
For always being there.
This poem is just to let you know
That all my life through,
I'll be so very grateful
I have a Dad like you

~~~

Dad is a word that says so much
It has a happy, special touch.
It means protection, love - fun too,
The kind of word made just for you

Funny Easter Verses

Some Easter poems are religious,
And some Easter poems are funny,
Some are all about Jesus,
And some, the Easter Bunny.

~~~

Well, this one is neither,
It's just an Easter greeting
To say - have a nice day,
With lots of chocolate eating.

~~~

It's nice to celebrate Easter
But here's a quiz for you:
Why don't we also celebrate
Norther, Souther, and Wester too?

Here's to the Easter Bunny,
Here's to the Easter Chick,
And here's to so much chocolate
It almost makes you sick.

~~~

So what does Easter mean these days?
Chocolate eggs and hot cross buns,
Some time off work, School Holidays,
Jesus of Nazareth reruns.

Religious Easter Poems

Jesus sacrificed himself
For all the wrongs we do.
He came to Earth and died for us,
So we'd be born anew.

~~~

Easter taught me my Saviour lives,
He's waiting there for me.
Let us go and walk with him
Into eternity.

Get Well Soon Poems

Sorry to hear that
You are feeling queasy.
We all understand that
Being sick ain't easy.

~~~

When I heard you were poorly
I thought "I think I'll get her
A card to send best wishes
That she will soon be better."

~~~

I know that you're not often ill,
It's once in a blue moon.
So here's a card to say that I
Hope you get well soon.

~~~

I hope you're not too ill.
I hope you get some rest.
I hope it won't be long before
You are back to your best.

Staying in bed all day
Sounds easy enough.
It's going back to work
That really will be tough.

Thank You Poems

General Poems to say Thank You

Thank you for your kind act
Which I will not forget;
You're one of the nicest people
That I have ever met.

~~~

Thanks for what you did for me,
You did not have to do it.
But I glad you did because
It helped me to get through it.

Birthday Gift Thank you

It's just what I have always wanted.
For years it's been something I covet.
So thank you for my birthday gift,
I really, really love it.

You really shouldn't have
You're a naughty such and such.
You spent far too much money,
But thank you very much.

~~~

Thank you very much
For the great gift that you bought.
It was very generous and I
Appreciate the thought.

Thank you for looking after my pet

Thanks for having [pet name]
He had a real nice time.
He wanted to get you a gift, but
I knew you'd prefer this rhyme.

...or, if you have got a gift:

Here's a little gift from [pet name]
He just wanted to say,
Thanks for having him while [your name]
Was off on holiday.

Poem to say thank you for your hospitality

Hello it's me again.
I just wanted to say
Thanks for your hospitality
I had a lovely stay.

Teacher Appreciation Poems

A poem for a Maths Teacher

Mathematics isn't easy but
I know it has its uses
(Except for that bit about
Squares and hypotenuses).
So this boy/girl wants to thank you
For teaching him/her hard sums,
It's bound to come in handy
Whatever he/she becomes.

A poem for an English / Poetry Teacher

We both know that poetry
Has never been my forté,
But I wanted to thank you,
And this seemed the best way.
I know what you are thinking -
"There's hope for him/her yet!"
But don't get too excited,
It's from the internet.

A Poem for a Science Teacher

I have enjoyed your class this year,
Your teaching is terrific.
Thanks to you I have become
A lot more scientific.

A poem for a History Teacher

I just want to say thank you,
In a little poem,
For teaching me of Vikings,
Greeks, and Ancient Rome.

A poem for an Art Teacher

I love the stuff you teach me,
The knowledge you impart,
You're really good at teaching,
You've made it a fine art.

A poem for a French Teacher

When people ask if I speak French,
From now on, I'll say "Oui."
So this is just a verse to say
Thank you, or, "Merci".
I don't know if I'd cope if
I ever went to France,
But now, thanks to you I know
I'd have a fighting chance.

A poem for a Spanish Teacher

You are a great teacher and
I've really loved your class,
So this is just a verse to say
Thank you, "Gracias".

General Teacher Appreciation Poems

You've been an awesome teacher
And I just want to say,
If I could grade you
You would get an 'A'.

I really love your class,
It really helps me grow.
You are a great teacher
The best one that I know

Funny Wedding Anniversary Poems

Funny Wedding Anniversary Poems for a husband or wife

I just want to tell you,
In this anniversary jingle
My love for you is stronger than
My yearning to be single.

~~~

Today's the perfect day
To act all smug and go
Out and belittle all
The single folk we know.

~~~

Let's celebrate, shall we,
The anniversary
Of the day that you gave up
And settled, for me!

Thanks for all the loving things
That you say and do.
Thanks for being my best friend,
Thanks for being you.
Thanks for being so thoughtful,
And showing that you care.
Thanks for being faithful
(As far as I'm aware).

~~~

Sometimes I lose my wallet,
Sometimes I lose my head,
One time I lost my car keys,
And had to walk instead.
Sometimes I lose the remote control,
I lose my temper too,
But there's one thing I'll never lose
And that's my love for you.

Funny Wedding Anniversary Poems for a couple

I've always hated couples,
Always, that is, until,
I met the pair of you, you almost
Never make me ill.

~~~

Your first anniversary!
Let's give a mighty cheer,
Because it's quite unlikely
I'll remember it next year.

~~~

You are a sweet and lovely pair,
It's beautiful - the love you share.
Sorry if this poem's sappy,
I'm just glad you're both so happy.

Sentimental Wedding Anniversary Poems

Sentimental Anniversary Poems for a husband or wife

I am so glad we chose each other
Out of all the rest.
I have always known that we
Would love each other best.

~~~

We've shared so much together
I can say without a doubt,
My feelings for you are stronger now
Than when we were going out.

Sentimental Wedding Anniversary Poems for a couple

It's clear that you were destined
To be husband and wife.
And now it's clear that you both have
A best friend for life.

~~~

I hope today that you look back
With happiness and pride
At the many cherished years
That you've spent side by side

~~~

You are our favourite couple
We think you're really great.
Congratulations to you both,
Go out and celebrate.

Funny Retirement Verses

I hear you are retiring.
How does it feel? Tell us.
On second thoughts, don't;
You'll only make us jealous.

~~~

"Youth is wasted on the young",
Or so I have been told.
But I reckon retirement
Is wasted on the old.

~~~

Say goodbye to the rat race,
Office politics, and tension.
Say hello to freedom,
Relaxation, and a pension.

~~~

I hear that you're retiring,
That's cause for celebration.
Why can't I retire too?
That's age discrimination!

Is retiring better than work?
I'll give it to you straight -
The pay is not as good but
The hours are bloody great.

~~~

I hope that you have fun
Being a retiree.
Enjoy those golden years
Being an OAP.

~~~

Roses are red,
Violets are blue,
I wish I was
Retiring too.

~~~

Retirement is here at last,
Toil and stress are in the past.
Now you can focus on that one thing...
I don't mean your family - I mean your golf swing!

Sad to hear you're going
You will be a great loss.
Glad the decision was yours
And not that of the boss.

~~~

Now that you are leaving
I finally can say
Everyone is glad, we never
Liked you anyway.

Sentimental Retirement Verses

Now that you are finally retiring
We're going to miss you so much.
We know that you will have a great time, but
Please promise us you'll keep in touch!

~~~

Over the years you have been an inspiration,
We all regard you with respect and admiration.
Now that your career has come to an end,
I will miss you, my colleague and my friend.

Good Luck Poems

General Good Luck Poems

I thought I'd wish you good luck, but
It's something you won't need,
Because you've something better -
The talent to succeed.

~~~

You'll be brill
I know you will.
You can do it,
There's nothing to it.
You'll be fine,
It's time to shine!

~~~

I know that you can do it,
I know you have the power.
You know, I really think that this
Could be your finest hour.

Good Luck For Exams

"A special set of skills"
That is what you have got,
And they will help with your exams
You're going to pass the lot.

~~~

Here's a note to say
We wish you all the best.
We know that you can do it so
Try not to get too stressed.

For a job Interview

Hope your interview goes well -
Best wishes and good luck.
I know that you're the greatest
Those other guys all suck.

~~~

You have the talent for this job,
You shouldn't have to beg.
But I suggest, if things turn bad,
Flash him a bit of leg.

~~~

You know I think that you would make
The perfect employee.
So let's hope that the interviewer's
Gullible like me.

~~~

Good luck for tomorrow.
I hope that you get hired.
I also hope it's years before
You're subsequently fired.

For a New Job

New beginnings are
Exciting but stressful.
I am quite certain though
You'll be happy and successful!

~~~

A new job is nerve-racking but
Please be calm, don't fret –
You know no-one, that's true, but also
No-one hates you yet.
And when you mess things up
(As you are surely bound to do)
Don't forget to say you're not
Incompetent, but new.

Printed in Great Britain
by Amazon